Chinese and Russian Military Artificial Intelligence: Drivers of National Goals

Chinese and Russian Military Artificial Intelligence: Drivers of National Goals

Brigadier Pawan Bhardwaj

(Established 1870)

United Service Institution of India

New Delhi (India)

Vij Books

New Delhi (India)

Published by

Vij Books
(Publishers, Distributors & Importers)
4836/24, Ansari Road
Delhi – 110 002
Phones: 91-11-43596460
Mob: 98110 94883
e-mail: contact@vijpublishing.com
web : www.vijbooks.in

First Published in India in 2024

ISBN: 978-81-98063-65-6

Contents

Introduction

Artificial Intelligence (AI) has demonstrated the potential to transform modern warfare and military operations. There is an evolutionary shift in warfare, from attrition-based approach to the one based on rapid and accurate decision-making, deployments, and precision destruction of the adversary's fight ability. It enables rapid decision-making in dynamic information-dense environments and extracts strategic information from the high-volume data. AI can revolutionise logistics, administration, maintenance, training, personnel management, and even routine activities. Additionally, AI improves military's ability to handle undefined war situations or hostile environments.

Since AI can deliver accurately and consistently, countries have created specialised AI systems to align performance with national goals. AI brings new opportunities to overcome unknown challenges in modern warfare and military operations. Global contenders are investing in this technology to establish their dominance in the power play, even tweaking existing algorithms from commercial applications to find uses in the military domain. This paper attempts to analyse the connection between military AI and national goals for China and Russia, drawing lessons for India.

Militaries around the world have employed AI with varied degrees of success. The associated control structures differ for each country, typically adopted to suit contextual capabilities and national goals. Russia and China stand out as existing examples for a study (though there are many more). Both countries are geopolitically active and provide a sufficient framework for the development and induction of AI tools, aligned with their global ambitions. Importantly, both nations share several strategic similarities, making their experiences particularly relevant for comparative analysis.

Firstly, China and Russia are large continental countries with vast and diverse populations. This diversity necessitates a nuanced approach to integrate AI into their military forces, accounting for varied linguistic, cultural, and regional differences. The terrain, climatic conditions, and border security challenges are comparable to those of India. These similarities provide valuable insights into managing diverse military needs across the operational environment. Secondly, both China and Russia maintain non-expeditionary military forces with a focus on regional defence and strategic deterrence, unlike the western model, which often involves large-scale expeditionary capabilities. This philosophy emphasises optimising limited forces with AI to enhance effectiveness and efficiency. Their methods offer a distinct perspective on leveraging AI for robust regional defence without extensive overseas engagements. China and Russia are also known for their subtle and strategic manoeuvres in international relations and military actions, offering non-lethal and non-contact 'Use Cases' where AI technologies have been implemented earlier to solve problems or achieve particular objectives. Their use of AI in cyber warfare, information operations, and asymmetric tactics provides critical lessons for countries facing similar challenges.

The Indian National AI Mission is expansive and contemporary, aiming to establish responsible AI prowess. A detailed analysis of the mission in the context of Indian military AI is useful for establishing an alignment with national goals.

CHAPTER 1

Global Artificial Intelligence Trends

Military AI is broadly sequenced into collection and analysis of surveillance data feeds, using multiple sources and sensors to detect and track objects or personnel. This is followed by analysis, where the available data is processed by Machine Learning (ML) to identify intentions, anticipate resource requirements, and plan associated training and mission enablers. During the operational conduct, AI provides real-time assessments to improve mission outcomes, efficiently targeting the adversary while protecting its own assets and information.[1] Concurrent, expeditious, and fail-safe processes are critical for operational sustenance. Military operations are grouped under the following classification for this paper and deliberated in the subsequent paragraphs.

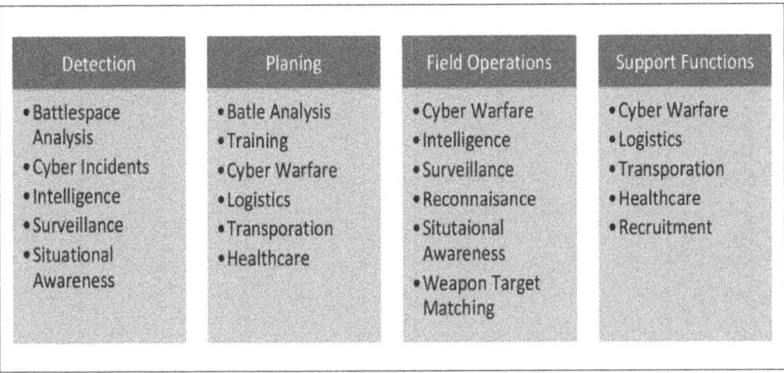

Figure 1- Taxonomy of Military Operations

Battlespace Analysis. To stay ahead of the information loop, militaries and nations conduct this analysis continuously, and not necessarily during a conflict situation. AI assistance provides wide-ranging and strategic insights during this stage. This analysis investigates reports, documents, newsfeeds, and other forms of unstructured information to gain an in-depth understanding of potential adversaries.[2] AI plays a crucial role by scrutinising large volumes of data and extracting useful information. The technology is assistive in assembling connected data across several datasets and various sources. It recognises patterns and derives correlations, providing a thorough grasp of the operational domains. The analysis also includes probability-based forecasts.[3] It wargames the success probability of mission alternatives and predicts enemy behaviour, weather and environmental conditions and potential supply line bottlenecks or vulnerabilities. Importantly, it can suggest risk mitigation strategies. Natural Language Processing (NLP) is capable of multilingual speech recognition[4] and translation in noisy environments. It improves military communication, especially in out-of-area contingency operations beyond traditional battle spaces. The computer vision geo-locates images without the associated metadata, fusing 2-D images to create 3-D models, and building tools to infer a pattern-of-life analysis (an important aspect for precise and surgical operations). All in all, the AI consolidates multiple inputs for timely, gap free analysis.

Intelligence, Surveillance, and Reconnaissance (ISR). As a precision activity, ISR is conducted to acquire battlespace initiative. It is specific to a space and time continuum and is highly focused. It is repetitive and requires revisits to the area of interest. ISR is conducted as a cross-domain activity, where AI scours digital media and unmanned systems, deployed along predetermined paths, assess threats over an extended period. This information processing is crucial in supporting military operations. Real-time, multisensory threat monitoring support is crucial for ML algorithms to track and identify targets from noisy data. AI can create increasingly realistic photo, audio, and video deepfakes[5] as part of information operations. These deepfakes influence public discourse, erode public trust, and are used for blackmail. The same AI also develops forensic tools to detect and counter such manipulations.

Situational Awareness. Soldiers in battle need battlefield intelligence and awareness to assess the tactical environment around them. This awareness will help soldiers undertake pre-emptive and precision actions to defeat the adversary. Battlefields are chaotic and create combat isolation, and the soldiers must be aware of their surroundings to take appropriate actions without delay. AI provides this real-time information, helping them to understand the complex situations and make better decisions. Unmanned systems play an important part in reading the battle space continuously, integrating relevant data and communicating a potential threat to military response teams. Furthermore, the integration of AI in target recognition can increase accuracy in the challenging combat conditions. AI decision support system provides real-time analysis and insights, assisting in informed decisions.

Targeting. This is the ultimate test of the military combat. It involves identifying targets, matching weapons, precision engagement, damage assessment, and re-targeting, if necessary. At this stage, the most prized output of a military AI is precision, lethality and, speed to destroy the adversary. AI target identification systems predict enemy activities, analyse mission[6] approaches, aggregate environmental data and employ countermeasures to enemy mitigation techniques. AI creates a single source of information, the 'Common Operating Picture', by fusing data from sensors across all domains of air, space, cyberspace, sea, and land. This comprehensive picture[7] provides decision-makers with a real-time analysis of friendly and enemy forces, and even offers a range of viable courses of action, potentially improving the quality and speed of wartime decision-making.

Autonomous Vehicles. Autonomous vehicles have a vast range and are likely a subject for another research paper. These vehicles are capable of operating without human input. They use a combination of sensors and actuators, supported by AI to sense their environment, make decisions, and control their movements. With a variety of payloads, these vehicles perform many tasks and operate on land, sea, under water, or air. The semi or fully autonomous vehicles are highly useful in dangerous or undesirable battle spaces. Attach a range of weapons to these autonomous vehicles, and they become Lethal Autonomous Weapon System (LAWS). A special class of weapon systems, these use sensor suites and computer algorithms to independently identify a target and engage it without human intervention. These systems are crucial for military operations in communication-degraded or denied environments, where traditional systems are unable to operate. Swarming[8] is a subset of autonomous vehicles that involves large formations of vehicles designed for a variety of tasks. Swarms can be non-lethal, precise, and silent, or lethal and loud. These swarms enter combat areas, cross international boundaries undetected and attack stealthily. Such swarms of drones, controlled from remote locations overwhelm the enemy countermeasures and can unleash unprecedented destruction.

Training and Simulation. The entire military chain of command can be trained using AI systems, which are increasingly employed in analysis, planning, decision-making, and physical training. AI can test or validate military concepts and plans. Realistic and virtual simulations create life-like scenarios to train soldiers, preparing them for real missions in a safe environment. AI training tools have shown a 40.0 per cent reduction in training time.[9] Scenario generation algorithms produce many environment options, including variations in terrain and enemy tactics, providing military planners with a wider range of war gaming exercises. War gaming analysis predicts outcomes of different training scenarios, highlighting areas that need improvement.

Transportation and Logistics. Military success depends on the effective movement of troops, equipment, ammunition, and supplies, for which AI is highly useful. AI reduces manual labour and transportation costs while detecting anomalies and predicting component breakdowns or supply chain congestions.[10] AI-induced predictive maintenance and analysis[11] extract real-time data from embedded sensors to determine when inspection or replacement is needed. AI provides guidance and navigational advice over uncharted terrain in the contested electromagnetic spectrum battlefield. Autonomous vehicles can travel great distances to drop off or pick up soldiers.

Cybersecurity. Cyberspace is now recognised as an integral component of military operations, permeating all domains and dimensions. Cybersecurity threats can cause severe damage, including the loss of critical military data. AI-based intrusion detection systems classify network activity as either normal or intrusive. Autonomous AI systems, trained to detect AI-induced anomalies, provide a more dynamic and robust defence. However, malicious actors are also aware of these AI defences and adapt their codes to evade detection. AI systems outperform humans in defending against unauthorised access to networks, programs, data, and computers. Additionally, AI monitors, records, and analyses patterns of cyberattacks, enabling the development of specialised countermeasures.

The Future of Military Decision-Making. Militaries worldwide generally adhere to the sequencing outlined in this chapter, with some following it rigidly and others more flexibly. AI processes vast amounts of data in real time, generating insights that facilitate swift and even pre-emptive decision-making, thereby disrupting traditional military structures. Effective militaries will harness AI's nonlinear capabilities to achieve more successful outcomes. Future-oriented forces will leverage AI to employ non-lethal, non-contact strategies, pre-empting the need for lethal combat.

Though the conceptual employment remains constant across countries, some modify and prioritise its use in a contextual framework. This monograph will study the Russian and Chinese militaries to highlight such priorities.

CHAPTER 2

Russia: Military Artificial Intelligence Philosophy

Russia is putting substantial efforts into closing the AI gap and staying relevant in the world, with the aim of improving operational effectiveness and efficiency. There are concerns, though, about integrating the archaic Soviet systems with modern and efficient data analysis. The automation of entire military command-and-control processes is still under development. The military officials understand the problem of a deep mismatch between the organisational and technical dimensions[12] of information support for combat operations and are working to resolve it.

AI Development Curve

Russians noted deficiencies[13] in robotic development well before outlining the AI roadmap by a specially directed campaign and launched a prospective military robotics program. They have organised annual conferences since 2016, entitled 'Robotisation of the Armed Forces of the Russian Federation' to document the disparity and interdepartmental coordination. The Advanced Research Foundation (ARF) was created to ensure superiority in defence technology and to warn the leadership about associated risks due to technological lethargy.

Russia's official AI strategy was unveiled in 2017, and it outlines a plan to become a global leader in AI by 2030. It recognises the potential risks and includes measures to address these concerns as well. The strategy focuses on three main areas of technological infrastructure: regulatory framework that encourages innovation and investment in AI, fostering a skilled workforce trough collaboration between government, academia and industry to achieve these goals.

In Mar 2018,[14] Russia brought the ministries of defence, education and science with the Russian Academy of Sciences to develop AI. This proposal sought to create AI and big data consortium to combine national efforts and establish a fund. The educational system of the proposal organised conferences to discuss AI proposals at domestic military forums and monitor global developments, and training system organised wargames to validate AI tools. AI and drone[15] design competitions also involve private players and developers. A national centre for AI is checking for compliance at the federal level. Russia also realises the importance of legal framework[16] to eliminate any development barriers.

Era (Russian for 'Good') Military Innovation Technopolis on the Black Sea is a dedicated AI research campus. This centre leads military research on AI, robotics, and automation. The centre will consist of a research, education, and a production cluster[17] to build prototypes; it is hoped to be a one-stop shop for all things Military AI.

Russia has a unique AI development strategy.[18] It is not led by the government nor by the private sector, but by state-owned firms. Sberbank, a state-owned retail bank, created the National Strategy in Oct 2019, an AI Roadmap in Nov 2019 and AI Federal project in Aug 2020. Rostec (a military hardware producer–also state-owned), Yandex (largest privately owned tech firm), and Gazprom Neft (fourth largest oil producer) are collaborating with Sberbank on the AI development. This unusual arrangement exists to distribution of the research and development across all participants to avoid duplicate efforts and encourage cooperation without conflicts of interest. Yandex launched Alice, an AI-enabled virtual assistant, and signed big data and ML contracts with Gazprom Neft in 2017. Rostec has successfully repurposed AI into its product development plans, working on AI-related technologies like 5G, blockchain, and Internet of Things devices.

Russian Military AI Strategy

Russian theorists delineate the elitist nature of AI from programming-based, uncomplicated algorithms. They believe that an inability to understand the essence of AI can hinder the development of true AI. This differentiation is expected to increase focus on AI development, without fear of unknowingly accepting a product or service with exaggerated capabilities, marketed as 'AI' (AI Whitewashing[19]), which is made to appear more sophisticated or intelligent than it is.

VM Burenok[20] articulated this concept clearly in a military journal in Apr 2021. His article proposes a wide-ranging role for AI in future military confrontation. AI data analysis can be used for forecasting and projecting politico-military situation, characterising and predicting actions by potential adversaries, and the resultant armed conflict. This technology utility provides a focus to military development. During the research and development stage, AI can assist in projecting possible weapons, their design deliberations and preventing accidents during both development and employment. Information warfare is a standard AI use case across multiple media and realms in all forms, through variety of tools. Cyberspace has a wide scope to utilise AI for pre-emption, as well as defensive and offensive actions. During combat, Russia supports the use of AI in reconnaissance, monitoring, and information support to process the complete combat picture. Russian

AI decision support systems aim to predict an adversary's actions during the combat cycle. Utilising nano-robots and swarms to launch shock reconnaissance (reconnaissance by fire to incite adversary to divulge his locations in retaliation) is a unique and interesting application. Russia wants to develop interactive and intuitive command and control and intelligent information systems. These systems are expected to have live environmental feedback to assess the situation and subsequently control diverse forces and assets in real-time. Russian robotic complexes (combat robots) with various levels of autonomy are expected to create greater mass during various contact battles. Finally, AI is expected to have utility in the technical planning and execution of operational and tactical logistics as well.

Trials in Syria

Russia tested 600 new weapons, including 200 next generation[21] military equipment in combat conditions in Syria achieving varying degrees of success. The unmanned vehicles performed a wide variety of tasks[22] in Syria, proving the Russian concept of robotic warfare. During 2018, Russia operated 60 to 70 drones daily, logging 23,000 missions and 1,40,000 flight hours.[23] The drones conducted aerial reconnaissance, target designation, and search and rescue. Russia also learned the importance of a specialised cadre for command and control of these weapons and equipment. The air and space forces[24] (*Voenno Kosmicheskie Sily*) was created to handle all responsibilities of development, construction and deployment of such weapons and equipment. A new concept of operations also exists for this equipment across the military.

Support during reconnaissance and fire support missions was provided by 22 Uran-9 robot tanks alongside infantry and engineer units. Russian battle robots captured the strategic tower of Syriatel[25] (Latakia province) in Mar 2016 in support of the Syrian army. It was the first-ever attack by a man machine team employing six Platform-M and four Argo Robots. Acacia, a self-propelled autonomous artillery system, destroyed enemy positions. The Andromeda-D system linked all military robots, guns, and drones to an automated C^4I^2 (command, control, communications, computer, intelligence, and information) system. While the tactical commander of the attack on the tower directed operations, operators of military robots sitting in Moscow led the attack, each aware of the battle field and the overall picture. Interestingly, the robotic complexes were never utilised for independent tactical manoeuvres, as was previously perceived. Sensor data generated by the vehicles did not provide complete battlefield awareness[26] to the operators in Moscow. This indicated the absence of AI systems capable of orientation and independent combat analysis.

Uran-6, a demining robot, successfully assisted military engineers in clearing recaptured areas from mines, improvised explosive devices, and unexploded ordnance. In Mar 2017, Uran-6 helped the Syrian government to clear the historic world heritage site of Palmyra[27] of 3,000 explosive devices across 2.3 sq km left by the Islamic State (Islamic State, formerly known as the Islamic State of Iraq and Syria/Islamic State of Iraq and the Levant). Russian engineers also employed Scarab and Sphere[28] during demining operations in Palmyra. Scarab is a small, wheeled platform with a high-resolution video camera, microphone, and thermal imager, controlled via a digital radio channel that provides surveillance video on a console to the operator. Sphere is a ball with four video cameras with light emitting diode lighting, a microphone, and an information transmitter that provides a 360-degree view. Its built-in positioning system automatically takes a vertical position after being deployed, allowing it to be lowered into wells and underground communications, thrown through windows to remotely inspect a room for suspicious objects.

Russia also tested an Unmanned Underwater Vehicle (UUV) in Feb 2018, when Galtel[29] was deployed to search for undersea unexploded ordnance, conduct seafloor mapping, and protect Russia's naval base at Tartus.

Battle Space Analysis

Russia, like many other countries, is investing in big data analysis to gain insights into complex problems and improve decision-making. Several initiatives promote the development of big data technologies and encourage their adoption by businesses and public organisations. The Digital Economy Program is one such initiative, aimed at developing digital infrastructure and improving access to data. The program also includes a national big data platform to enable data sharing and collaboration across different sectors. Leading technology companies, such as Yandex and Mail.ru, are investing heavily in big data research and development to analyse vast amounts of data quickly and accurately, enabling data-driven decisions.

Communication metadata and content—including phone calls, email traffic, and web browsing activity—are accessible to numerous federal agencies in Russia. Civilian tech companies are also developing facial recognition and speech recognition technologies with potential military applications. One example is the System for Operative Investigative Activities, which provides lawful interception[30] of all communications, including internet, to federal agencies. Another facial recognition software, called FindFace[31], is used in Moscow's extensive urban surveillance network. This system allows the authorities to monitor the daily movements of almost 12 million people.[32]

Similar technologies can be employed in urban conflict when combined with data from unmanned systems and enhanced by AI algorithms. These will improve the Russian military's situational awareness in urban settings and enable effective information operations in cities by tracking individuals and identifying potential targets. AI, in conjunction with these technologies, will process large amounts of data in real-time enhancing the military's ability to respond to complex situations.

Information Operations

Future conflicts will employ a variety of resources, possibly blurring across the grey zone of diplomatic, informational, economic, and military lines. As with other countries, Russia will utilise AI to gain an edge in this grey zone. Information warfare is a central tenet of contemporary conflicts and a useful strategy for advancing foreign policy goals.

The Apr 2007 cyberattacks against Estonia were a series of distributed denial-of-service attacks in response to the Estonian government's decision to move a Soviet-era war memorial from a central square in the capital city of Tallinn. The attacks overloaded the Estonian government websites and disrupted critical online services such as banking and media outlets. This resulted in the disruption of critical infrastructure, of which Russia obviously denied any involvement in. In the 2008 war between Russia and Georgia, the Georgian government's various ministries, departments, and news agencies were subjected to attacks, leading to the unavailability of their web material. As a result, Georgia had to rely on alternative servers to host its online content. Online surveys conducted during the time suggested that Russia's actions were perceived as peacekeeping. Similarly, blog entries were also found to be more in favour of Russia than Georgia.

Today, any individual with a smartphone and access to the internet can share real-time images, videos, and other content that can reach and influence millions of people across the globe. In this new information ecosystem, information operations and public affairs functions have become increasingly important for the success of the mission.

AI, especially generative AI, can create deceptively realistic but not necessarily true depictions of events. This can be utilised as a tool for election manipulation, as reported during the Trump victory. The East StratCom Task Force[33] has also noted that Russia has used AI based deepfakes to gain political footholds across the globe.

Command and Control

Russia has a historical inclination to use mathematical models, and other quantitative tools to support military decisions. *Raketno-Yadernoye Napadenie*[34] (Nuclear Missile Attack or RYAN), a mathematical computer model was developed in the early 1980s to calculate the overall strategic balance between the then Soviet Union and the United States (US). At a certain degree of imbalance, RYAN would suggest a preemptive nuclear strike to the leadership. This mathematical model has eased the ingress of AI into the command, control, and decision support systems. Activated in 2014, the National Defence Management Centre[35] (*Natsional'nyi Tsentr Upravleniya Oboronoi*) provides a common operating picture for Russia. It is expected to employ AI to collect, collate, and always analyse information on the military-socio-political situation across globally.

Russia has also established a variety of smaller military command-and-control systems. These include individual and tactical systems for various branches of the armed forces and, most importantly, the Automated Command and Control Systems[36] (*Avtomatizirovannaya Sistema Upravleniya*) in the military districts and the National Defence Centre. Another system, the Reconnaissance Strike Contour (RSC)[37], is designed to coordinate the employment of high-precision, long-range weapons. It is linked to real-time intelligence data and provides precise targeting to a command and control centre. The RSC is designed to function at operational depths using surface-to-surface missile systems and aircraft-delivered smart munitions.

Electronic Warfare (EW)

Currently, Russia has a range of highly mobile EW systems in its arsenal. Russia's interest and emphasis on EW is clearly triggered by satellite communications, Global Positioning System (GPS) navigation, and high-bandwidth internet dependence of American and North Atlantic Treaty Organisation (NATO) militaries, and hopes to supress their decision-making abilities, creating a domino effect on the battlefield forces.

The RB-109A Bylina is a fully autonomous system[38] that analyses combat situations, identifies targets, determines how to disable them, and ultimately issues orders to EW forces in the field. After deployment, Bylina[39] automatically establishes communication with the higher headquarters, tactical command posts in field and individual EW stations. It recognises radio stations, communication systems (including low-powered ones), radars, early warning aircraft, and enemy satellites almost immediately upon deployment and effectively resolves complex radio-electronic environments without human intervention. It can take AI-enabled decisions and suppress or jam adversarial stations. The Russian deployment of Bylina in the Donbas region of Ukraine in 2018, gained favour with the military, which increased EW efficiency by 40 to 50 per cent.[40]

Military Robots

Russia is investing substantial resources into the development of unmanned systems, evidenced by the numerous Unmanned Aerial Vehicles (UAV), Unmanned Ground Vehicles (UGV), and UUVs in various stages of research and testing. These systems are primarily operated remotely, but greater autonomy can be achieved as software technology improves. By incorporating AI into semi-autonomous and autonomous vehicles, it is possible to enhance force protection, situational awareness, and the ability to navigate complex urban terrain. Russia has prioritised the robotisation of on-board fire resources creating robotic strike complexes (*Robotekhnicheskie Kompleksy*), which can also be grouped into specialised assault units – all with aim of reducing losses and increasing effectiveness by increasing their strike capabilities. Although currently operated in remote mode by an offset soldier, in the future, they would function independently of humans, taking into consideration the system's current state and the external environment. In the future, Russia will seek to completely automate the battle[41] and introduce robotic groups capable of conducting independent warfare. This adaptive capability will allow them to self-adjust under changing conditions and AI is expected to execute fire missions under real combat situations. The Russian robotic landscape is analysed in the following paragraphs.

Nerekhta. It is a multifunctional, modular tracked robot. Its variants include a fire support module (equipped with a 12.7 mm or 7.62 mm machine gun), a reconnaissance module for artillery, and a transport version designed to deliver equipment and ammunition during engagements. It can navigate to predetermined targets without the need for a remote operator. It is considered an ideal platform to serve as a testbed for a host of military AI applications,[42] including collaborative behaviour with other systems.

Kamikaze[43] **Nerekhta**. The versatile chassis is designed to approach the target and detonate itself, much like a suicide bomber. The operator uploads a map into the system, selects the target and launches it on its mission. The Nerekhta will plot its course to the target, approach it and blow it up. Future versions will allow for multiple uses, enabling the robot to approach the target, place an explosive device on it and retreat to a safe distance for reuse.

Platforma M. This system is designed for visual and technical reconnaissance as well as fire support during patrolling, reconnaissance, detection and destruction of enemy equipment. It includes a 7.62 mm machine gun and four RPG 26 anti-tank grenade launchers.

Soratnik. The BAS-01G Soratnik (Comrade-in-arms[44]) is an unmanned armoured tracked ground vehicle designed for reconnaissance, fire support, patrols, and the protection of important facilities. It can operate in conjunction with other automated combat units.

Uran 9. This unmanned tank is designed to destroy mobile targets, buildings, and installations. It can be operated by remote control or can function autonomously or set on a pre-programmed path[45] for combat operations. Weighing 10.0 tons, its modular structure includes 23 mm and 30 mm automatic guns, 7.62 mm Kalashnikov tank machine gun, six rocket-propelled flamethrowers, and an anti-tank missile system. It is also equipped with a variety of sensors, laser warning systems, thermal, and electro-optic cameras. Russia is also considering the export of the Uran 9.

Vikhr. It provides fire support during urban reconnaissance operations and the destruction of lightly armoured targets. It can be fitted with multiple modules, such as 30 mm cannon, coaxial tank machine guns, Kornet anti-tank missiles or a 57 mm automatic cannon. It also carries four quadcopters that can be used for Kamikaze attacks on high-value targets. Notably, its targeting data can be used by aviation, artillery, and other robots as well.

Shtrum. Near-urban combat missions in Syria have not been considered completely successful,[46] and Russia is working on changes to withstand challenging conditions. Project Shturm[47] (Storm), based on the T-72 tank chassis, will include four combat vehicles and a mobile command centre capable of operating within a radius of 3 km.

Volk 2. It is an unmanned, tracked assault reconnaissance vehicle. It can detect and destroy stationary and mobile targets, provide fire support and protection to important facilities in automated security mode. It can be equipped with either a 12.7 mm or a 7.62 mm machine gun or a 30 mm automatic grenade launcher. It features a laser rangefinder, an armament stabiliser, a thermal imager, and an electronic ballistic computer. In its automated mode, the operator can remotely select up to 10 targets, which the robot then engages.[48]

Taifun-M. A tracked security robot designed for the protection of strategic missile facilities, is a unique concept expected to be autonomous, it will be a fail-safe option to guard strategic missile sites hosting the RS-24 Yars and SS-27 Topol-M missile.[49] Weighing 900 kg it can operate continuously for 10 hrs with a speed of 45 kmph. It has cameras, a laser rangefinder, and radar sensors to monitor the strategic site, and a 12.7 mm heavy machine gun to engage the hostile targets.

Msta-SM 2S19M2. This is an AI-enabled robotic artillery system with an automated guidance and fire control system for howitzers, using smart high-precision shells. The combat vehicles can exchange information[50] among themselves regarding each shot fired, leading to more efficient usage of firepower and better coordinated attacks.

Armoured Fist. This AI system will sift through vast quantities of satellite imagery[51] and control all airborne and land-based assets for optimal data analysis and decision-making. The system will convert data from all national early warning radars, anti-aircraft, and anti-missile systems, analyse the information, and reach faster conclusions for launching long-range precision missiles (S-300 and S-400).

Lantset. Known as Kamikaze variety, with a 3 kg payload, it can hit a target within a 40 km radius. The drone can transmit a live image of the target, confirming the success of the strike on target. Its high speed of 300 kmph can destroy a wide variety of enemy UAVs.[52]

Altius. This AI-enabled bomber UAV can operate independently and interact with 5th generation aircraft, such as the SU-57. As a wingman, its AI enhances command and control, navigation autonomy, target identification, and target engagement. Once it receives the coordinates of the target, Altius determines the optimal route to the target, drops bombs, and returns to base without the assistance of an operator.[53]

S-70 Okhotnik-B. This heavy stealth combat UAV, in automated mode, is interoperable with Su-57 lead aircraft.[54] The lead human pilot is expected to fly alongside a swarm of UAVs, increasing the combined aerial mass.

Argo Amphibious Vehicle. This Jeep-sized amphibious vehicle can cross lakes to conduct reconnaissance and deliver support fire for amphibious landings and perform tactical load delivery[55]. It is armed with a 7.62 mm tank machine gun, antipersonnel grenades and rocket launchers.

Underwater Mini Torpedoes. AI will control these slow-moving mini torpedoes in groups.[56] Travelling at just 2 to 3 mph, they will be silent and inconspicuous. AI will alter their movement patterns to resemble a school of fish. This unique concept has unlimited uses and probably high lethality.

Poseidon Autonomous Underwater Vehicle. Expected to dive deeper and travel faster, it can destroy all types of surface vessels and can carry either a conventional or potentially a nuclear warhead.[57] It can lie idle on the seabed within target range (such as an aircraft carrier or a city), awaiting attack instructions.

Unicum. This control system can communicate with ten robots simultaneously. It can guide a selected robot to the most favourable position and search for the target, which a remote operator can then engage. The on-board AI is expected to protect the system from malware, viruses, and false commands information. It can also transfer its environmental awareness to other robotic devices.

Marker. This UGV is capable of functioning autonomously, using a neural network to create swarms on the battlefield. It also serves as a testbed[58] for computer vision, autonomous movement, navigation, and swarming technologies.

Swarm Technology. The Russian military has shown interest in swarm robots[59] coordinate through networks, able to act in a formation under human control. Civilian industry is also developing a UAV swarm for independent combat operations to penetrate enemy territory and strike targets.

Final Experimental Demonstration Object Research. This is the first Russian anthropomorphic armed robot capable of space[60] travel. It is designed to replace humans in high-risk areas and is trained in a variety of tasks in an urban environment.

Robotic Urban Warfare.[61] Russia has also developed a concept for urban robotic warfare. The Russian concept utilises robotic assault formations (Robotic *Robotekhnicheskie Kompleksy* - RTK) to improve success in lethal urban environments, as outlined below:

- An RTK assisted attack would consist of a combined reconnaissance (utilising multiple sensor suites) and fire support by a light ground robot (with anti-shrapnel protection) and an aerial UAV.

- Heavy RTKs (featuring tank-type armour protection and direct firing capability) would provide artillery fire to support the penetration advance and destroy highly protected targets.

- Specialised remote controlled RTKs would create passages through obstacles under the cover of medium RTKs (*Boyevaya Mashina Pekhoty* [Battle Infantry Fighting Vehicle] styled protection and fire support). This group would also protect flanks, hold captured regions and provide addition fire support to heavy RTKs.

- Light RTK (anti-small arms protection) would destroy enemy personnel, unarmoured equipment, and defend command posts.

- Transport RTKs would provide battlefield and tactical mobility during the operation.

Russia aims for its military robots to be faster, more discerning in target selection, and more accurate than human soldiers, while operating alongside them. The country's approach focuses on retrofitting and enhancing existing platforms with robotic capabilities, rather than developing entirely new systems. These robots are expected to react more swiftly to sensor data, acquire precise targeting information, and execute tasks with increased precision. Russia believes that the outcome of intense battles will be influenced by minimising human casualties, an area in which it seeks to achieve significant results.

Advancements in military robotics, autonomy, ML, and AI are expected to enhance intelligence collection and analysis, facilitate navigation and manoeuvring in hazardous terrain, enable precise targeting, reduce the costs of urban warfare, and improve combat effectiveness across various military operations. Russia is developing a broad range of unmanned systems and aims to refine these tethered and semi-autonomous robots with AI-driven C^{4}ISR (command, control, computers, communications, computer, intelligence, surveillance and reconnaissance) capabilities. These technologies are intended to protect soldiers' lives and enhance the precision and lethality of combat forces. Russia's focus on robotics is designed to counterbalance the softer, algorithmic AI approaches of its traditional adversaries, such as NATO and the US.

CHAPTER 3

China: Military Artificial Intelligence Philosophy

Chinese Self-Assessments and Military Concepts. Reference to Chinese Hanzi-scripted morphemes is inevitable when analysing any document, especially those involving policies and military concepts. 'Self-Assessments' are of special interest here, reminding the world of the internal state analysis and justification of every action. In 2015, one such assessment called 'Five Incapables'[62], the People's Liberation Army (PLA) emphasised unsettling incapability of some officers, who cannot judge situations, cannot understand higher authority's intentions, make operational decisions, deploy troops successfully or deal with unexpected situations. Earlier in 2009, 'Peace Disease' assessment had acknowledged poor combat experience over four decades. Blaming officer's 'Do not expect to go to war' attitude who took shortcuts and underwent 'Go through the motion' training, PLA now seeks to 'Cure the peace disease' and prepare to 'Fight to win'.

Developing Military Warfighting Concepts. In line with developing military warfighting concepts, 'Potential Ways' are discussed in China too. Exploratory papers also mention of 'Intelligent Combat' with 'Superior performance beyond the limitations of the human body', capable of providing new tools and thus new ways of warfighting.[63] China's obsession with creating new phraseologies is evident in these newer concepts. Latent warfare refers to pre-deploying unmanned systems (much like human deep assets) near important enemy targets, keeping them in a long dormant state, to execute attacks at the appropriate time. Cluster warfare (another term for swarming) employs large number of intelligent, unmanned, and autonomous systems in a coordinated manner for reconnaissance or combat to overwhelm the enemy. Global rapid strike warfare utilises hypersonic speeds, space, and unmanned combat platforms to precisely attack enemies across the globe within an hour. Chinese security thinkers have grouped the emerging technologies to formulate novel combat concepts and provided a vision roadmap to its developers and military.

Ban on Lethal Autonomous Weapon Systems. Though China has proposed a ban on[64] LAWS, its version of a definition is too narrow and does not constrain homegrown development or use. This pathological need for China to play with words is a way to tire out negotiators and prolong discussions and harass the adversary. While China is aggressively developing robots, it is likely to focus more on the digital and virtual domains than on the physical realm. It is careful to avoid being trapped in an arms race and suffer the experience of the former Soviet Union. Advanced data processing and decision support systems will identify hidden enemy systems, understand their vulnerabilities, and turn sensor data into a common operating picture. Under conditions of informatised warfare, large-scale attrition of enemy forces is not a priority objective; it is, in fact, to dominate the adversarial military systems. The PLA would attempt to create disruption or paralysis on the enemy side by targeting operational systems and disabling them. Following this concept[65], China would rather bank on algorithms and unmanned platforms to precisely target enemy's underbelly (software and hardware) rather than a full-spectrum, distributed warfare.

AI in Cognitive Warfare. It is highly probable that the PLA will utilise AI in cognitive warfare, which involves disinformation[66], misinformation, and propaganda strategies. This approach is consistent with the conventional Chinese military philosophy, which emphasises the importance of winning over the hearts of the people and subduing the enemy without resorting to direct confrontation. AI makes it more precise, undetectable, and omnipotent.

Blitz Attack on Taiwan. A small visualisation on blitz attack[67] on Taiwan is noteworthy. PLA may take advantage of its proximity and America's geographical distance from Taiwan to speed up its attack. It will attempt to demotivate American intentions to come to Taiwan's rescue. There could be a combination of AI at rest (algorithms, cyberattacks, and battle network systems) and AI in motion (unmanned systems and precision-guided missiles) to exploit this relative advantage window and gain full access/area denial.

Chinese AI in Intelligence, Surveillance, and Reconnaissance. It is also noteworthy that 20.0 per cent of Chinese AI efforts revolve around ISR, which has wide-ranging applications in geospatial imagery analysis, media analysis, and intelligence acquisition. The PLA's Strategic Support Force[68] (PLASSF) now split and reorganised as the Information Support Force[69], is leading the way in acquiring geospatial information, perception, and intelligent analysis subsystems. China's AI strategy aims to enable its platforms to quickly locate hidden targets and fuse multiple intelligence sources, including UAVs, open-source intelligence and human intelligence, into a single, comprehensive operating picture.[70] Their aim is to combine the output of space-based, airborne, and terrestrial sensors to enable autonomous monitoring and post-strike damage assessments of large areas across the world.

AI-supported Space Operations. China is exploring AI-supported analysis to manage large satellite constellations[71] for space operations. Its smart radio technology will improve space-based communications by autonomously shifting channels, while autonomous satellite operation will compensate for limited communication windows and bandwidth. This approach will reduce the workload of ground satellite operators. By collaborating with satellites and utilising sky wave over-the-horizon radar[72], UAVs can effectively locate and monitor hostile targets and instantly relay the collected data. As a result, Chinese military UAVs will play a crucial role in the kill chain during anti-aircraft carrier operations.

Overcoming Operational Inexperience through Hybrid Intelligence. The PLA is ready to use AI in war-gaming and simulation to train military officers. Institute of Automation at the Chinese Academy of Sciences in Beijing has built AlphaWar[73] for such a military exercise. In 2020, experienced military strategists could not identify the presence of AlphaWar during a test experiment. Unknown to human strategists, it provided sound military decisions, sometimes superior to those made by humans. It is also capable of self-learning. Unlike board game AI (such as AlphaGo), military wargames are different, since they include many intangibles, the fog of battle episodes, and human behaviour. AI and fuzzy logic fit into military systems to guide to navigate the intangibles and generate more comprehensive military strategies, and AlphaWar seems to be heading that way.

Autonomous Command Decision Making. The PLA is actively exploring the use of AI to enhance situational awareness in support of decision-making, particularly in response to its self-analyses of the five capabilities. By leveraging AI, the PLA seeks to evaluate the potential consequences of various courses of action, thereby achieving decision superiority in future intelligentised warfare.[74] The focus is on improving cognitive speed in decision-making, particularly in high-speed operational environments. There is a priority on the development and implementation of AI-based solutions to enhance future command decision-making capabilities. As a mind-machine interface, AI is expected to organise the inputs in a more understandable manner for commanders to make decisions. The importance of integrating and leveraging synergies among human and machine hybrid intelligence is expected to support command decision making in many ways[75], both concurrently and sequentially, or perhaps, in some contexts, even replace human commanders on the future battlefield.

Overcoming Operational Inexperience through Hybrid Intelligence. China's conceptual integration of hybrid intelligence into its military decision-making is a way to overcome operational inexperience. Analysis of previous events is considered a vital aspect of the concept for better command decisions in future. This AI would highlight priority recommendations based on the predicted success percentages of a decision outcome. This would help commanders make more objective and scientific decisions by sorting through large volumes of data, removing chaff, and encouraging attention to priority inputs. Even if a 'Decision Support System' does not materialise, the AI-developed strategies or plans would provide an opportunity to identify and correct flaws in human plans, provide more than one option, and allow military commanders to think beyond usual practices.

Enhancing Command Decisions with AI. Given its inadequate combat experience or joint operations, the PLA considers AI an 'Indispensable Digital Staff Officer' during planning and execution. For a quick battle resolution, China desires AI to analyse all operational inputs simultaneously, identify the operational bottlenecks and windows of opportunity, and recommend reinforcement for a specific line of operation. AI will also automate target selection, proving more proficient than humans at striking multiple targets simultaneously. Cyber, ballistic missile defence and defence of critical infrastructure are areas of concern where the pace of operations surpass the human ability to intervene effectively. Consequently, autonomous systems may be delegated greater autonomy to defend such systems.

Electronic Warfare. AI-powered UAVs are expected to distinguish and categorise electromagnetic signals using ML. These UAVs fly over enemy territory to disrupt the enemy's electronic equipment, air defence, and fire control radar, bolstering China's attack capabilities.[76] By detecting and classifying signals from radar and communication systems, AI-enabled UAVs can follow efficient anti-jamming protocols.[77] This special interest in EW resonates with similar Russian concepts of operations. The focus on EW is driven by the US and NATO militaries' heavy reliance on satellite communications, GPS navigation, and high-bandwidth internet. China will aim to disrupt communication and decision-making capabilities to reduce the effectiveness of battlefield forces.

Cyber Warfare. The cyber/network domain entails categorising large amounts of data in real-time to identify threats and update defences, where AI systems will improve the speed and scale of cyber defence.[78] AI-guided navigation of adversary's networks will be useful during technical reconnaissance and cyberattacks. The PLA is researching the use of pattern recognition to identify and defend against distributed denial-of-service attacks and to identify advanced persistent threats. China is also researching deep neural networks to detect intrusions. Cyberattacks are in consonance with the Chinese concept of attacking the vulnerable underbelly of the adversary.

Predictive Maintenance and Logistics. The PLA Air Force is utilising image recognition to identify cracks in engine propellers and impeller blades for quick repairs. Another application analyses many data points from equipment and maintenance to indicate predictive maintenance[79] for each piece of equipment separately, optimising human effort. The same application will also predict failures in electromechanical systems. Big data and data analytics are expected to improve the supply chain by indicating disruptions to enhance acquisitions and maintenance processes. During 2020–21, over 11.0 per cent of the 343 AI contracts were focused[80] on maintenance, repair, logistics, or sustainment. China is insisting that all contractors to provide AI-based detection for fault diagnosis and smart warehousing.

Airborne Robotic Systems. Not shying away from kinetic options, China has inducted a wide variety of AI-in-motion systems including robotic unmanned systems and precision-guided missiles, to prepare for kinetic options during symmetric, asymmetric and cyberspace warfare. While PLA Rocket Force wants to create full-fledged remote sensing and target identification, the PLA Strategic Force[81] is focusing on AI for its electronic, cyber, space, and psychological warfare. China is also concentrating on autonomy to improve the effectiveness of existing platforms and tactics. Functional UAVs have enhanced China's confidence to conduct reconnaissance and surveillance to protect claimed territories. In the early 2010s, for the first time, BZK-005 unmanned reconnaissance aircraft flew over Diaoyu Dao, part of Senkaku Islands disputed area, while avoiding

Japanese detection. Information during competition and conflict is important[82] and a large array of UAVs given below fill up that role magnificently for China:

- **EA-03 Xianglong**. This is a high-altitude, long-endurance unmanned reconnaissance aircraft. With a mission load of 600 kg and an effective range of 7,000 km, it can conduct continuous aerial surveillance for 10 hrs from an altitude of 1.8 km.

- **Attack-1**. Equipped with synthetic aperture radar, laser-guided missiles, and GPS-guided bombs, this can operate continuously for 20 hrs at a maximum speed of 370 kmph.

- **JWP02 (ASN-206)**. This carries out a tactical unmanned reconnaissance with a range of 150 km.

- **BZK-005**. A stealthy medium and high-altitude long-range unmanned reconnaissance aircraft, which has an endurance of 40 hrs.

- **Dark Sword**. Unveiled during the Zhuhai Air Show in Oct 2012, it caught the world by surprise. It is stealthy, supersonic, ultra-high mobility aircraft which can autonomously perform air-to-air combat, ground attack and carry anti-ship ballistic missiles. It is the world's only aircraft carrier attack UAV system.[83]

- **Star Shadow** This is a stealthy combat UAV with a radar cross-section of 1 sq ft.[84] It is a blended-wing and twin jet-engine platform, having endurance of 12 hrs, a cruising speed of 600 kmph, and an altitude ceiling of 40000 ft.

- **The GJ-11**. Known as the Sharp Sword[85], it is a UAV designed as a stealthy flying wing vehicle. This drone can take off from warships without human intervention and carry out various tasks, such as releasing swarming decoys or EW equipment, launching guided weapons, and conducting aerial surveillance missions.

Manned Unmanned Teaming. With advanced air defence weapons, many supported with full autonomy, China understands the vulnerability of manned aircraft. Complementing manned aircraft with UAVs is an obvious solution. By deploying sensors and radars further away from the manned aircraft, the UAVs can serve as pathfinders, greatly reducing pilot casualties. Fully autonomous UAVs, supported by advanced navigation technology, will no longer be mere remote-control models, thereby reducing the cognitive load on the manned aircraft pilots in hybrid teams. This will free pilots to undertake higher-function roles, such as executing fire missions. UAVs and manned aircraft will leverage their respective advantages, complementing one another while evolving in tandem.

Ground Robotic Systems. The PLA held a 'Dangerous Crossing'[86] contest in Sep 2018, to develop cutting-edge, next-generation contextual systems. The contest featured competitions in cross-country reconnaissance, cross-country formations and transportation, air-ground collaborative reconnaissance, realistic walking drones designed to follow and support troops, and UGVs capable of conducting transportation missions across mountainous terrain. Two the most interesting concepts, discussed below, indicates clear preference of UAVs over UGVs:

- **Sharp Claw 1**.[87] It is a six-wheeled, reconnaissance vehicle, has been in service with the Chinese military since 2020, though the numbers are not known. Possibly autonomous, it weighs 120 kg, has a small profile, and lends itself to logistics roles since it is mounted with a single machine gun only.

- **Sharp Claw 2.**[88] It is an unmanned 6x6 wheeled UGV for battlefield reconnaissance, patrolling, assault and transport missions. In addition to carrying weapons and ISR accessories, it can transport a smaller Sharp Claw 1 mini UGV. Its electric motor allows the vehicle to move silently across extreme terrain. It can be remotely operated but has autonomous mission functions, especially when approaching an objective.

Maritime Robotic Systems. To overcome the communication clutter and significance of 'Timely and Just' nuclear launch commands, the PLA Navy (PLAN) nuclear submarines are being equipped with an AI decision-support system to 'Reduce commanding officers' workload and mental burden'.[89] The AI submarine is expected to receive communication signals and interpret those using convolutional neural networks. In addition, the Navy is looking for autonomous vehicles for a variety of roles discussed below:

- Shanghai University has developed a series of autonomous under surface vehicles to monitor and map long coastlines. These vehicles can navigate complex terrains, avoid obstacles such as reefs, icebergs, and other moving vessels. Key features include intelligent autonomous control and marine target detection and recognition.[90] It identified a new anchorage while working with a polar research vessel in Antarctica. It also detected and sampled contaminated water after the sinking of the oil tanker Sanchi in the East China Sea. China is exploring the integration of swarm intelligence to enable cluster control and cross-domain synergy between the sky, land, and sea, with ongoing research focusing on deep-sea exploration and long loiter time.

- China has deployed a fleet of slow moving, but long-endurance underwater drones known as the Sea Wing (*Haiyi*) Glider[91] in the Indian Ocean and Selayar Islands in the Flores Sea of Indonesia. Using Variable-Buoyancy Propulsion,[92] these slow-moving underwater drones are considered high-value naval intelligence tools. Similar gliders are used by the US Navy too. PLAN and Yunzhou Systems are conducting autonomous swarm testing on these drones to improve their capabilities. Sea Wing is expected to support submarine operations during military missions with AI support to interpret underwater acoustic signals for target recognition.

- The D3000[93] is a stealthy warship designed to operate autonomously for months. It can operate independently or in conjunction with manned ships for long periods. Its four sets of seven barrelled, 30 mm rapid fire guns, drone launch decks, anti-ship missile launchers and torpedo tubes makes it one of its kind at sea. The US considers it a prime example of China's rapid AI technology development.

- Reports also suggest that, massed unmanned systems could disrupt enemy communications and subvert anti-submarine capability. These underwater drones could act as a decoy and pull the adversary into an ambush.[94]

Swarming. To overwhelm the adversary's battlefield awareness, China has invested heavily in developing swarms across all physical domains. Chinese swarms are well-suited for ISR, communications, and strike missions. The possibility of developing air-launched, retrievable collaborative swarms[95] to simultaneously strike high-value targets is a special area of interest.

Future Ready China

The Chinese government has a well-known ability to devote substantial funds to AI development. China recognises that collaboration between the public and private sectors is a key to technological leadership. It is urging private companies to develop critical technologies like AI, and is even providing subsidies.[96] The private sector is unlikely to invest in risky, long-term research, which makes government funding crucial. The Chinese government's capacity to signal priorities to the private sector and local governments is also advantageous. The government is trying to address talent and growth issues by recruiting highly educated officers[97], enlisted personnel, and civilian staff, effectively competing with the private sector.

In 2023, China validated AI's capability to design[98] the electrical system of a warship '300 times faster' than the traditional method. It is claimed to be accurate, as it learns from a database of Chinese ship design knowledge and decades of past experience. New designs are rechecked with the existing databases to ensure accuracy. This AI system operates with guidance from humans. Fast ship launches, despite this AI trial, are already a concern for the US Navy; "One shipyard has more capacity than all of our shipyards combined" observed Navy Secretary Carlos Del Toro. The Indian Navy Chief also notes that the construction speed of China has resulted in the launch of 148 warships[99] in the last 10 years, almost the size of the Indian Navy.

CHAPTER 4

India: National Artificial Intelligence Mission

In Jan 2018, the 'Task Force on AI for India's Economic Transformation' recommended steps for AI transformation in India. Consequently, National AI Mission was launched in Mar 2024 as one of nine missions under the Prime Minister's Science, Technology and Innovation Advisory Council (PM-STIAC). This overarching council is mandated to advise the PM on action-oriented and future-preparedness of the government. The PM-STIAC missions are wide-ranging to include natural language translation, quantum frontier, national biodiversity mission, electric vehicles, bioscience for human health, waste to wealth, deep ocean exploration, and accelerating growth of new India innovation.

The National AI Mission is led by the Ministry of Electronics and Information Technology (MeitY).[100] It focuses on benefiting India's societal needs at large, specifically targeting healthcare, education, agriculture, smart cities and infrastructure, smart mobility, and transportation, an extension of 'Making AI in India and Making AI Work for India'. It is intrinsically linked to achieving nine out of the 17 United Nations sustainable development goals of eliminating poverty, establishing good health and well-being, providing quality education, creating decent work and economic growth, increasing industry, innovation, and infrastructure, reduce inequality, mobilise sustainable cities and communities, influence responsible consumption and production, and build partnerships for the goals.

The AI Mission will receive INR 10,300 crore starting from the Financial Year 2023-24 till 2027-28. To harness the Indian expertise in management and science, the services of the Digital India Corporation (DIC), a not-for-profit organisation set up by the MeitY is running the AI Mission through 'IndiaAI' Independent Business Division. DIC seeks judicious mix of talent and resources from the government and the market for successful and timely delivery of the national missions. A structured implementation through a public-private partnership model will boost the AI innovation ecosystem. There is natural division of the components[101] addressing the large AI ecosystem, collaborating rather than competing within and with each other. Each of the seven collaborating components, function with dedicated initiatives and integrate with each other, aligned to transformational AI growth as follows:

- **IndiaAI Compute Capacity**. Understanding the need for high-end computing, this pillar will build a high-end scalable AI computing ecosystem to cater to the increasing demands from expanding AI start-ups and researchers. The pillar will comprise 10,000 or more Graphics Processing Units (GPUs), built through public-private partnership. As the importance of 'Owning compute facility' grows, global technology giants with deep pockets are attempting to control vital AI computing assets. Microsoft invested USD 1.0 bn (2019) and USD 10.0 bn (2023) in Open AI, while IBM invested USD 6.5 bn (2022) in research.[102] An AI marketplace will also be designed to offer pre-trained models and AI as a service to innovators, acting as a one-stop shop. AI is an expensive enterprise, and India wants to optimise hardware and software infrastructure to support AI computation. This pillar has specific initiatives for tangible goals. AI Research, Analytics and Knowledge Assimilation for Transformation (AIRAWAT), National Supercomputing Mission, and MeitY Quantum Computing Applications Lab offer many such development options for startups and researchers.

- **IndiaAI Innovation Centre (IAIC).** As a leading academic institution, IAIC will streamline implementation and retention of top research talent. It will spearhead the development and deployment of foundational models, with a specific emphasis on indigenous Large Multimodal Models and domain-specific models, leveraging edge and distributed computing (and restricting uncontrolled language models) for optimal efficiency. The special emphasis on edge and distributed computing indicates contextual architecture needs and is an important guiding beacon for the ministries and military.

- **IndiaAI Datasets Platform.** This pillar will utilise a unified data platform to enhance access to high-quality non-personal datasets. There is a special emphasis on enhancing the accessibility, quality, and utility of public sector datasets to assist data-driven governance. Reliable and available data will fuel the development and capabilities of AI, enabling insights, predictions, and intelligent decision-making. Related initiatives in this component include the Data Management Office, India Datasets Program, and India Data Platform.

- **IndiaAI Application Development Initiative.** This component will promote AI applications in critical sectors for sourcing problem statements from central ministries, state departments, and other institutions.

To democratise the solutions and coordinate development initiatives, a common problem statement documentation resource will improve efficiency and delivery mechanisms. This component will also serve as a repository of common use cases for others to emulate. The initiative will focus on 'Developing, scaling, and promoting adoption of impactful AI solutions with potential to catalyse large-scale socio-economic transformation'. Recognising intellectual property and innovative practices as major confidence-building mechanisms, this component intends to support new developers, ensuring proprietorship of their respective products. Related initiatives include AI Centres of Excellence, National Centre on AI, and MeitY Startup Hub, which will assist in AI intellectual property and innovations mechanisms, procedures, and control.

- **IndiaAI FutureSkills**. This component will provide the skills and education for AI programmers. By democratising and standardising AI skills, developers will obtain entry into undergraduate, masters-level, and doctoral programs. Data and AI Labs in Tier 2 and Tier 3 cities across India will create wide foundational skillsets by expanding the reach of AI education. Related initiatives in this component include Future Skills Prime, Transformation of Industrial Training Institutes/Polytechnics, and Responsible AI for Youth.

- **IndiaAI Startup Financing**. This pillar will support and accelerate deep-tech AI startups and provide them streamlined access to funding to enable futuristic AI projects.

- **Safe and Trusted AI**. Recognising the need for adequate guardrails, India is advancing the responsible development, deployment, and adoption of AI. This pillar aims to create indigenous solutions for standardisation, self-compliance, governance, and audit. As part of AI ethics and governance, it will develop and guide the responsible and transparent deployment of AI systems to ensure fairness, accountability, and societal benefit. It supports initiatives such as Digital India Bhashini and India Stack.

Chapter 5

Correlation of National Goals and Military Artificial Intelligence

Russian Case

In Jan 2024, NATO launched Exercise Steadfast Defender 24, involving 90,000 service members from 31 NATO allies and Sweden. Aimed at testing the rapid deployment of forces to reinforce the Euro-Atlantic area through the trans-Atlantic movement of forces from North America, it was also meant to demonstrate unity, strength, and determination.[103] Russian Deputy Foreign Minister Alexander Grushko described it as an irrevocable return to the Cold War alliance.[104] Russia has repeatedly mentioned NATO incursions in the neighbourhood as a threat to its sovereignty. It is not a surprise that Russia has prioritised the development of combat robots (though not yet fully autonomous), underpinning its adversarial concern for NATO on western borders. Continuing this premise of national threat perception, the military AI development in Russia is summarised and analysed below:

- Russia conducted a detailed analysis of the existing deficiencies that could delay AI development. This self-analysis also promotes the 'Islands of Excellence' and starter hubs for a faster and more reliable development cycle, a mature approach adopted by most militaries.

- Out-of-military structures like ARF have been established to observe and advise the governments on the non-linear nature of adversarial attempts. Russia's drive to ensure defence technology superiority and to warn the leadership about the risks of technological lethargy contrasts with the corporate-driven military technology development in the US.

• To counter the deep financial resources of the US defence industry, Russia selected Sberbank, a state-owned retail bank that holds one-third of all bank assets in Russia, to develop a national strategy in Oct 2019, an AI roadmap in Nov 2019, and an AI federal project in Aug 2020. This unique approach allows AI development to be led by state-owned enterprises rather than the government or the private sector.

• A National Centre for AI has been established to develop and implement AI solutions, ensuring compliance. Russia is acutely aware of the geopolitical risks associated with non-compliance issues, which could hinder its AI advancements, and has put safeguard mechanisms in place.

• Russia tested over 600 new weapons in combat conditions during the Syrian conflict, across various tasks, serving as a proof of concept for its tactical and operational capabilities. The use of remote and radio-controlled systems indicates Russia's focus on functionality over advanced technology, with an expectation to improve AI systems through practical application. The Syrian battlefield also provided valuable adversary response data across the physical, informational, and cognitive domains.

• Russia is highly attuned to the cognitive capabilities of its major adversaries and has deployed systems to legally intercept all forms of communication among its citizens.

- AI-powered cyber defence and offence systems, in collaboration with civilian-military sectors, further showcase Russia's sensitivity to adversarial capabilities.

- AI-enabled, highly mobile EW systems have been developed to target satellite communications, GPS navigation, and the internet dependencies of US and NATO forces. The goal is to disrupt decision-making abilities and create a domino effect on battlefield operations.

- Russia employs AI to study adversaries, although this is not publicly acknowledged. AI collects and fuses data from multiple sources, filtering out irrelevant information. 'Pattern of Life Analysis' is a significant outcome of this process and plays a critical role in ISR efforts, indicating Russia's areas of concern.

Chinese Case

China's AI development is closely aligned with its national objectives, reflecting its aspirations for technological leadership. The breadth and depth of its AI initiatives reveal ambitions not only for civilian advancements but also for bolstering military capabilities. Military AI plays a crucial role in supporting China's strategic goals of becoming a regional leader and a rising global power. China aims to enhance its military capabilities, deter potential adversaries, and assert its influence in international affairs through the following key actions:

- Triggered by geopolitical considerations and the need for changes in military and national policies, China has undertaken deep internal studies. Of particular interest are the 'Five Incapables' and 'Peace Disease' studies, which highlight poor combat experience and the necessity to improve Human Resource (HR) capability.

The focus on advancing AI for autonomous systems in command decision-making, EW, cyber warfare, and predictive maintenance is designed to mitigate human limitations. In contrast, China is strategically positioning itself to engage in conflict and achieve victory at any cost.

• AI is expected to be employed in all scenarios, especially in newly coined combat scenarios such as latent warfare, cluster warfare, and global rapid strike warfare, to overwhelm adversaries.

• Private Chinese companies are developing critical technologies with financial support from government subsidies. They are actively recruiting (poaching) the best technologists from across the world. The urgency to acquire usable AI is a hallmark of a national objective of an aspiring global power.

• There is a special focus on cognitive warfare through AI-supported disinformation, misinformation, and propaganda strategies.

• Defining AI as a 'Digital Staff Officer' is a typical Chinese attempt to simplify AI to the most basic, understandable level and improve traction in the military. This philosophy also allows China to compensate for its lack of combat experience.

• The maritime domain has seen significant efforts, including the deployment of autonomous underwater drones for surveillance and strategic operations. China's emphasis on aerial UAVs indicates preparations for operations beyond its immediate region across vast seas and land borders against the US and NATO.

- Testing of slow-moving, long-endurance underwater drones (Sea Wing [*Haiyi*] Glider) and their autonomous swarm capability demonstrates China's interest in the wide Pacific Ocean.

- The D3000, a stealthy warship designed to operate autonomously for months, could also disrupt enemy communications, neutralise anti-submarine capabilities, or act as a decoy and lure adversaries into an ambush.

- Mountain-based robotic ground systems are expected to provide an added boost to operations against India's experienced and battle-hardened troops.

- China expects swarming AI systems to increase force mass and overwhelm adversary systems across the non-kinetic and kinetic spectrum.

- AI is expected to enhance wargaming capabilities in China, with a clear purpose to train its senior leaders in complex decision-making and overcome combat inexperience.

- China is utilising AI to perform complex design parameters and hasten its production capability. Routine tasks like electrical circuit designing are now allotted to AI for quicker and multiple options. This will reduce the development timelines of military systems, which is critical for force projection in the future.

- China is actively participating in international debates on ethics, governance, and compliance to book a seat at the high table of compliance and governance, tailors these debates to suit its own needs or prolongs discussions to create sufficient space for its own operations. Although China has proposed a ban on LAWS, its own definition is too narrow and does not constrain indigenous development or use.

Both China and Russia are aware of the vibrant military-industrial complexes of western countries and have found their own unique processes to remain competitive on the global stage. They are focused on implementing military AI in a way that is tailored to their specific strategic contexts. Both countries have developed unique homegrown solutions to address indigenous challenges, with differing processes in each nation. This approach represents a logical methodology for acquiring this novel technology without depleting national resources in a blind pursuit of military AI.

CHAPTER 6

Recommendations: Indian Military Artificial Intelligence and National Artificial Intelligence Mission

The Indian National AI Mission aims to establish a sovereign AI[105] and carve a niche for itself among the likes of Google and Meta. Consolidation of efforts to acquire costly GPUs, appropriate skill management, and developing applications will aid in in dataset and IP management. Public-private partnerships reflect an intent to utilise the best of both powerhouses for a common goal. When examining Indian Military AI initiatives alongside the broader AI mission, notable parallels and alignments emerge with some notable alignments. It would be prudent for Military AI to metaphorically 'Avian Draft' with the National AI Mission, benefiting from consolidated efforts. While this collaboration may seem counterintuitive to traditional military security principles, it will need to adapt and address these concerns for improved AI utility.

AI, an international subject, is susceptible to replication. However, the absence of a universal monitoring body makes this replication uncontrollable, posing a concern for AI developers in India. AI relies on regulated datasets for its functionality, and unless these datasets are secure, the country's security may be compromised. To address this concern, the government plans a National Data Governance Framework Policy to promote ownership safety and trust in non-personal data, with access restricted to designated and authorised offices. India also aims to safeguard against bias, discrimination, or compromise in the electoral process by labelling all artificially generated media and text with unique identifiers or metadata. In response to this concern, the Indian government issued an advisory in Mar 2024, mandating platforms to obtain explicit permission before implementing any 'Unreliable AI models/Large Language Model (LLM)/ generative AI, software, or algorithms' for users accessing the Indian internet. A subsequent clarification stated that the advisory only applies to 'Significant large platforms' and excludes startups. The focus of the advisory was on untested AI platforms deployed on the Indian internet, with social media intermediaries directed to utilise consent pop-ups to explicitly inform users about the unreliability of AI-generated data. This government advisory permits a fair amount of operating space for startups and smaller platforms and does not stifle the large but fragile startup enterprise base. These regulations mark the beginning of AI governance in India, a necessary step considering AI's growing significance in business and its potential for misuse.

The government's vision of #AIFORALL, coupled with unregulated dataset usage and controlled AI development, could lead to 'AI inflation' if not accompanied by appropriate regulations. This unchecked proliferation of AI technologies risks compromising quality, reliability, and ethical considerations, potentially undermining trust in AI systems and increasing associated risks. The concept of property rights in India differs from the global perspective, with *Daan* (donation) associated with community service—a unique characteristic of the Indian psyche. With this in mind, the *Bhasha Daa*n (language donation) initiative under the National Language Translation Mission aims to crowdsource translation models through open data and open-source software. Project Vaani, funded by Google at Indian Institute of Science, Bengaluru, and Applied Research in Technology and Humanities Park, also in Bengaluru, is one such project under *Bhash Daan*. The project encourages Indians to donate their language reading and writing skills to help create large training datasets for future NLP projects. India must be cautious of large technology companies potentially misusing these regulations and utilising community donations to fund their individual projects surreptitiously. Without sufficient regulations, donated datasets may become free raw material for commercial enterprises.

The military should leverage the available AI research platforms, AIRAWAT and the Param Siddhi AI System, to ensure cost-effective accessibility. The dedicated allocation and specialised consultations of these national assets offer AI as a service, representing a prudent decision. By co-sharing computational power, the military can harness on-demand resources without the need for significant investments in expensive hardware and infrastructure. The conversational AI provided under the scheme offers significant utility and encompasses a variety of applications, including automatic speech recognition, text-to-speech, and NLP, all of which are particularly relevant to military needs. High-bandwidth shared storage as a default quota to each project provides exclusive rights to the developers, thus alleviating the military information security concerns.

Combining *Meghdoot* cloud services with AIRAWAT and the procurement and supply chain management with AI system will create a sophisticated ecosystem for high-computing research across the military regions and country. National Supercomputing Mission (NSM)[106] addresses the increasing computational demands of academia, researchers, micro, small, and medium enterprises, and startups completing 73.25 lakh high-performance computational queries. The Indian military can utilise these facilities to train its personnel until its own captive facilities are established. NSM has proven its capacity to successfully install high-performance computing machines, completing 24.83 petaflops across the country, exceeding the original target of 15 to 20 petaflops. The Indian Army will also benefit from utilising 17,500 NSM trained specialists for proving and establishing its own facilities.

Engaging with the IndiaAI Datasets Platform represents an area where the military must reconsider its more reserved approach. The national dataset will be secured by the best minds and systems, over which the military can layer its own secure mechanisms. The India Stack and the associated infrastructure will be highly useful for military needs and should not be overlooked. Universal availability of such datasets will provide a broader operational landscape for all military endeavours. The Indian Air Force (IAF)[107] is already leveraging DigiLocker's secure and accessible document repository services. All service documents of IAF personnel can now be issued, accessed, and verified digitally in secure storage with easy retrievability.

Collaboration and engagement with the Indian Data Management Office will familiarise the army with the relevant data policies and guidelines established by this office. The streamlined data collection practices and systems, data integrity and accurate record-keeping, will assist the army in growing digitally and responsibly. India Datasets Program, now renamed as Open Government Data Platform India, provides clean and useful data for innovation. The portal offers various visualisations of data, allowing users to identify their needs and utilise appropriate data that boasts high non-fungibility. Additional benefits from newer techniques in data analysis, data cleaning, and quality assurance checks will also be useful for the army's growing needs.

AI Skilling is yet another facet where the military should leverage national resources. Whether it is IAIC, IndiaAI FutureSkills, or the IndiaAI Application Development Initiative, military will never be able to focus on AI skilling in isolation. As a disciplined force, it will be beneficial for the military to engage with the largest knowledge gateway of the AI mission in pursuit of its skilling goals. Partnering the military with technical schools of instruction and these pillars will create bridges of knowledge and HR. Already mentioned as a challenging enterprise, Indian fears misuse of unreliable LLM[108] and, thus, the military may also want to distance itself from their development, leaving it instead to IAIC. Specific emphasis on edge and distributed computing by this pillar will remain of particular interest to the military and may become a major collaboration point with national resources.

Trusting the IndiaAI Application Development Initiative will provide the military with greater flexibility to redefine its critical problem statements in collaboration with other governmental bodies and enhance the delivery mechanism. Identification of common problem statements and work methodologies will drive army technology absorption in consonance with the national pace and shared transformative growth.

The Digital Personal Data Protection Act, 2023 governs the processing of digital personal data in India, irrespective of its original format, and can address some of the privacy issues related to AI platforms. Complementing this is the Information Technology Act (Intermediary Guidelines and Digital Media Ethics Code, 2021), which oversees various entities, including social media intermediaries, over-the-top platforms, and digital news media. Section 66E of the Information Technology Act 2000 addresses privacy violations related to deepfakes and crimes associated with privacy breaches. Section 66D targets malicious use of communication devices or computer resources imposing penalties of imprisonment and fines. The IT rules require social media platforms to promptly remove such content, or they risk losing their 'Safe Harbour' protection. Military AI development in India must be mindful that even minor breaches could compromise national security by consolidating irresponsible datasets. There should be mandatory caution against developing AI products through unverified sources. Standardised security parameters should become crucial facets of military AI development, with a special allegiance to national digital infrastructure.

The military will have a major role to play in the safe and trusted AI component of the AI Mission. Interestingly, the Ministry of Defence is represented only by Defence Research and Development Organisation in the national mission, leaving out the Department of Defence and Department of Military Affairs. It will be cavalier to imagine that the AI ethics should be the sole prerogative of the developer and not the user or the planner. The debate over whether ethics in technology, particularly in the realm of AI, should be driven by users is crucial. Users are the ultimate stakeholders in AI technologies, and therefore should have a significant say in defining ethical standards. Developer-driven ethical standards based on the technical capabilities of AI systems, may make the system inherently weak, especially in the military arena. Since the decision to create an AI tool has been made with due deliberation, building additional constraints into the system will render it less useful in battle.

A comprehensive input from the Ministry of Defence, rather than a purely scientific outlook, would be highly appropriate. AI has both digital and physical aspects, thus, user participation at all levels of AI visualisation, designing, development and deployment will yield better benefits.

The Indian Army should collaborate with the National AI Mission's pillar of Safe and Trusted AI and create its own expert group on ethical standards for international discussions. This group will remain responsible for understanding the ethical standards in the correct perspective, suggest modifications to own systems to retain their edge in the battle space. Integrating ethics into military AI systems will mitigate risks, ensure compliance with moral principles, and enhance the overall quality and effectiveness of AI products. By prioritising ethical considerations, Military AI developers will demonstrate their commitment to upholding moral values, and societal norms, thereby justifying the usefulness of AI systems. This trust is essential for the widespread adoption and acceptance of military AI technologies, ultimately strengthening the battlespace. This proactive risk management will also reduce the likelihood of adverse outcomes and operational failures.[109]

Conclusion

The development of AI in the military sector is intricately linked with national goals and aims, especially in the context of perceived competition and conflicts. As nations strive to assert their influence, protect their interests, and maintain strategic dominance, AI emerges as a critical tool for achieving these national objectives. The intersection of AI and national objectives is evident in the strategic alignment of military modernisation efforts with technological innovation agendas, as illustrated by recent developments in Russia and China. AI initiatives in the military sector support these overarching objectives, whether it be deterrence, power projection, or regional aspirations.

As tensions rise and strategic rivalries intensify, nations will seek to leverage AI to gain competitive advantages, deter adversaries, and safeguard their interests. The development of AI-enabled weapon systems, cyber capabilities, and autonomous platforms reflects the competitive dynamics driving military innovation and strategic planning. The national context is shaped by perceived conflict environments, such as Russia's land border disputes with NATO and China's vast oceanic competition with the US, or perceived adversary vulnerabilities, such as NATO's high dependence on communication and technology, which both Russia and China exploit. Both nations are examining how to landscape, secure, and attack the cognitive domain to either destroy or moderate an adversary's will. They are also addressing their own vulnerabilities, such as Russia's lack of corporate development capability and China's under-experienced soldiers, through special measures like public sector-driven AI development in Russia and the aggressive recruitment of specialists in China.

As new technologies transform warfare and redefine strategic competition, nations must harness AI in a manner that is contextual to their own environment and people. No two nations will adopt a similar approach to AI development and induction. By aligning AI development with national security imperatives, nations can proactively address emerging threats, safeguard their interests, and shape the future contours of the global security architecture. This is a natural survival instinct, prioritising the development of AI tools in the manner that is most understood and effective for each nation. No country can afford to engage in out-of-context, prohibitively costly AI development activities.

By aligning AI initiatives with overarching strategic objectives, India too will find it advantageous to focus its efforts on fulfilling the National AI Mission. The Indian military, as an integral part of the nation, will benefit from aligning its efforts with the National AI Mission, enhancing military capabilities within relevant timeframes, asserting influence, and safeguarding national interests in an increasingly complex and contested landscape.

Endnotes

1   Nihar Dalmia et al., "The Age of With- The AI advantage in defence and security", Accessed on 15 Dec 2022.

    https://www2.deloitte.com/ca/en/ pages/deloitte-analytics/articles/ age-with-ai-advantage-defence-security.html

2   Eray Eliaçık, "Guns and Codes: The Era of AI-Wars Begins", Data Economy, 17 Aug 2022, accessed on 09 Dec 2022.

    https://dataconomy.com/2022/08/how-is-artificial-intelligence-used-in-the-military/#:~:text=Artificial %20intelligence%20is%20 used% 20in,driven%20systems%20in%20the%20military

3   Tejaswi Singh and Amit Gulhane, "8 Key Military Applications for Artificial Intelligence", Market Research, 03 Oct 2018, accessed on 23 Mar 2022.

    https://blog.marketresearch.com/8-key-military-applications-for-artificial-intelligence-in-2018

4   Congressional Research Service, "Artificial Intelligence and National Security", 10 Nov 2020, accessed on 11 Jun 2022.

    https://sgp.fas.org/crs/ natsec/R45178.pdf

5   Ibid.

6   Eliaçık, "Guns and Codes".

7   Congressional Research Service, "National security".

8   Manish Kumar Jha and Amit Das, "AI Technology in Military Will Transform Future Warfare", 13 Aug 2021, accessed on 10 Nov 2021.

    https://www.businessworld.in/article/AI-Technology-In-Military-Will-Transform-Future-Warfare/13-08-2021-400525/

9   Eliaçık, "Guns and Codes".

10   Shraddha Goled, "What Are The Scope and Challenges of Using AI in Military Operation", Analytics India, 01 Nov 2020, accessed on 23 Mar 2022.

https://analyticsindiamag.com/what-are-the-scope-and-challenges-of-using-ai-in-military-operations/

11   Congressional Research Service, "National security".

12   Pavel Luzin, "Artificial intelligence in the Russian Army", Riddle, 19 Mar 2021, accessed on 13 Feb 2023.

https://ridl.io/artificial-intelligence-in-the-russian-army/

13   Samuel Bendett, "Red Robots Rising: Behind the Rapid Development of Russian Unmanned Military Systems", Strategy Bridge, 12 Dec 2017, accessed on 18 Feb 2023.

https://thestrategybridge.org/the-bridge/2017/12/12/red-robots-rising-behind-the-rapid-development-of-russian-unmanned-military-systems.

14   Samuel Bendett, "Here's How the Russian Military Is Organising to Develop AI", Defense One, Jul 20, 2018, accessed on 15 Feb 2023.

https://www.defenseone.com/ideas/2018/07/russian-militarys-aidevelopment-roadmap/149900/

15   Samuel Bendett, "The Russian Military Wants Students to Design Its New Underwater Drone", 07 Mar 2028, accessed on 18 Feb 2023.

https://warisboring.com/the-russian-military-wants-students-to-design-its-new-underwater-drone/

16   Presidential Address to the Federal Assembly at Saint Petersburg, Russia on 01 Mar 2018, accessed on 18 Feb 2023.

http://en.kremlin.ru/events/president/news/56957

17   Aleksey Nikolsky, "Lofty Goals", Force India, accessed on 19 Feb 2023.

https://forceindia.net/cover-story/lofty-goals/

18   Lee Sullivan, "Artificial Intelligence in Russia", 20 Feb 2022, accessed on 19 Feb 2023.

https://geohistory.today/ artificial-intelligence-in-russia/

19 Bernard Marr, "Spotting AI Washing: How Companies Overhype Artificial Intelligence", Forbes, 25 Apr 2024, accessed on 10 May 2024.

https://www.forbes.com/sites/bernardmarr/2024/04/25/spotting-ai-washing-how-companies-overhype-artificial-intelligence/

20 Anya Fink, Book Review, Russian Studies Series 5/21, "Russian Thinking on the Role of AI in Future Warfare", Review of V.M. Burenok, "Iskusstvennyy Intellekt v Voennom Protivostoyanii Budushchevo" ("Artificial intelligence in the military confrontation of the future"),NATO, 08 Nov 2021, accessed 13 Feb 2023.

https://www.ndc.nato.int/research/research.php?icode=712

21 Bybelezer, C, "How Russia is using Syria as a military 'guinea pig'", The Jerusalem Post, 28 Feb 2018, accessed on 18 Feb 2023.

https://www.jpost.com/Middle-East/How-Russia-is-using-Syria-as-a-military-guinea-pig-543839

22 Margarita Konaev and Samuel Bendett, "Russian AI-Enabled Combat: Coming to a City Near You", War on the Rocks, 31 Jul 2019, accessed on 13 Feb 2023.

https://warontherocks.com/2019/07/russian-ai-enabled-combat-coming-to-a-city-near-you/

23 ibid.

24 ibid.

25 ibid.

26 Global Security, "Uran-9", accessed on 21 Feb 2023.

https://www.globalsecurity.org/military/world/russia/uran-9.htm

27 Rajesh Uppal, "Russia Deployed Family of Killer Robots", IDST, accessed 10 Feb 2023.

https://idstch.com/military/army/russia-developing-family-of-killer-robots-conduct-war-games/

28 Translated by Chat GPT, accessed on 21 Feb 2023.

https://ria.ru/20171017/1507003664.html

29 Samuel Bendett, Stephen Blank, Joe Cheravitch and Michael B. Petersen, "Russian Unmanned Vehicle Developments: Syria and Beyond", Research Report, Centre for Strategic and International Studies (CSIS), 2020, accessed on 16 Feb 2023.

https://www.jstor.org/stable/pdf/resrep24241.9.pdf?refreqid=excelsior%3Acb84ae3db9884c6124737659bae8e07b&ab_segments=&origin=&initiator=&acceptTC=1

30 Zack Whittaker, "Documents reveal how Russia taps phone companies for surveillance", 18 Sep 2019, accessed on 21 Feb 2023.

https://tcrn.ch/32MaCYb

31 Stephanie Petrella, Chris Miller, and Benjamin Cooper, "Russia's Artificial Intelligence Strategy: The Role of State-Owned Firms", FPRI, Orbis, pp 76, Volume 65, Issue 1, Nov 2020, accessed on 15 Feb 2023.

https://www.fpri.org/article/ 2021/01/russias-artificial-intelligence-strategy-the-role-of-state-owned-firms/

32 Konaev and Bendett, "Russian AI-Enabled Combat: Coming to a City Near You", ibid.

33 European Union External Action, accessed on 16 Feb 2023.

https://www.eeas.europa.eu/search_en?fulltext=artificial+intelligence

34 RAND, "Military Applications of Artificial Intelligence: Ethical Concerns in an Uncertain World", accessed on 24 Jan 2023.

https://www.rand.org/pubs/research_reports/RR3139-1.html

35 ibid.

36 Luzin, "Artificial intelligence in the Russian Army".

37 Bendett, "Russian Unmanned Vehicle Developments: Syria and Beyond".

38 Timothy Thomas, "Russia's Electronic Warfare Force- Blending Concepts with Capabilities", Sep 2020, accessed on 18 Feb 2023.

https://www.mitre.org/sites/default/files/2021-11/prs-19-2714-russias-electronic-warfare-force-blending-concepts-with-capabilities.pdf

39   Alexey Ramm Bogdan Stepovoy, "Sees the target: -- without the participation of the operator", 16 Apr 2020, accessed 16 Feb 2023.

https://iz.ru/1000101/aleksei-ramm-bogdan-stepovoi/vidit-tcel-bylina-smozhet-atakovat-protivnika-bez-uchastiia-operatora

40   Dr Margarita Konaev, "Military applications of artificial intelligence: the Russian approach", Chatham House, 23 Sep 21, accessed on 23 Mar 22.

https://www.chathamhouse.org/2021/09/advanced-military-technology-russia/06-military-applications-artificial-intelligence

41   Timothy Thomas, "Russian Robotics: A Look at Definitions, Principles, Uses, and Other Trends", MITRE, Feb 2021, accessed on 13 Feb 2023.

https://irp.fas.org/eprint/russian-robotics.pdf

42   Kelsey D. Atherton, "Is this Russia's gateway drone to better armed robots?", C4ISR Net, 31 Jul 2019, accessed on 17 Feb 2023.

https://www.c4isrnet.com/unmanned/2019/07/31/is-this-russias-gateway-drone-to-better-armed-robots/

43   Uppal, "Russia Deployed Family of Killer Robots".

44   Global Security, "BAS-01G Soratnik Comrade-in-Arms", accessed on 21 Feb 2023.

https://www.globalsecurity.org/military/world/russia/soratnik.htm

45   Uppal, "Russia Deployed Family of Killer Robots".

46   Konaev and Bendett, "Russian AI-Enabled Combat: Coming to a City Near You".

47   Andrei, "The robot was officially confirmed - Storm", Live Journal, Andrei-bt, 27 Sep 2018, accessed on 21 Feb 2023.

https://andrei-bt.livejournal.com/949786.html

48   Army Guide, "MRK-002-BG-57 Volk-2", accessed on 21 Feb 2023.

https://army-guide.com/eng/product5525.html

49   Army Recognition, "Taifun-M anti-commando vehicle fully operational in Russian Strategic Missile Forces", accessed on 21 Feb 2023.

https://www.armyrecognition.com/news/army-news/army-news-2017/taifun-m-anti-commando-vehicle-fully-operational-in-russian-strategic-missile-forces-tass-11601171?highlight=WyJ0YWlmdW4iLCJtIl0

50   Sharathkumar Nair, "A closer look at Russia's AI-powered artillery", 26 Jan 2022, accessed on 21 Feb 2023.

https://analyticsindiamag.com/a-closer-look-at-russias-ai-powered-artillery/

51   Konaev and Bendett, "Russian AI-Enabled Combat: Coming to a City Near You".

52   Roger McDermott, "Russian UAV Technology and Loitering Munitions", Real Clear Defence, 06 May 2021, accessed on 21 Feb 2023.

https://www.realcleardefense.com/articles/2021/05/06/russianuavtec hnology_ and loitering munitions_775980.html

53   Global Security, "Altair / Altius-M / Altius-O / Altius-U", accessed on 21 Feb 2023.

https://www.globalsecurity.org/military/world/russia/altair.htm

54   "Russian troops to start receiving Okhotnik strike drone in 2024 — official", TASS, 14 Apr 2021, accessed on 18 Feb 2023.

https://tass.com/defense/1277657

55   Uppal, "Russia Deployed Family of Killer Robots".

56   RAND, "Ethical Concerns".

57   Melissa Heikkilä, "AI: Decoded: Putin's high-tech war — Making sense of AI systems -Deepmind controls nuclear fusion reactor", 23 Feb 2022, accessed on 13 Feb 2023.

https://www.politico.eu/newsletter/ai-decoded/putins-high-tech-war-making-sense-of-ai-systems-deepmind-controls-nuclear-fusion-reactor-2/

58 "Iron Guard: Russia's Most Dangerous Combat Robots", RIA, 15 Oct 2017, accessed on 17 Feb 2023.

https://ria.ru/20171015/1506649786.html

59 RAND, "Ethical Concerns".

60 Uppal, "Russia Deployed Family of Killer Robots".

61 PA Dul'nev, "The Employment of Robotic Complexes During the Assault of a Town (Fortified Area)", Vestnik Akademii Voennykh Nauk (Journal of the Academy of Military Science), No. 3 2017, p. 27, referred by Timothy Thomas, "Russian Robotics: A Look at Definitions, Principles, Uses, and other Trends", pp 11, MITRE, Feb 2021, accessed on 13 Feb 2023.

https://irp.fas.org/eprint/russian-robotics.pdf

62 Dennis J Blasko, "The Chinese Military Speaks to Itself, Revealing Doubts", 18 Feb 2019, accessed on 10 Mar 2023.

https://warontherocks.com/2019/02/the-chinese-military-speaks-to-itself-revealing-doubts/

63 "The curtain of Era of Machine Warfare is opening", PLA Daily, 04 May 2017, extracted and translated on 10 Mar 2023.

http://www.xinhuanet.com//mil/2017-05/04/c_129588629.html

64 Forrest E. Morgan et al., "Military Applications of Artificial Intelligence", RAND, 2020, accessed on 24 Jan 2023.

https://www.rand.org/content/dam/rand/pubs/research_reports/RR3100/RR3139-1/RAND_RR3139-1.pdf

65 Yuan-Chou Jing, "How Does China Aim to Use AI in Warfare?", The Diplomat, 28 Dec 2021, accessed on 15 Dec 22.

https://thediplomat.com/2021/12/how-does-china-aim-to-use-ai-in-warfare/

66 SD Pradhan, "Transformation of the Chinese influence operations into a Cognitive war: Warning for India", The Times of India, 21 Jul 2022, accessed on 13 Mar 2023.

https://timesofindia.indiatimes.com/blogs/ChanakyaCode/transformation-of-the-chinese-influence-operations-into-a-cognitive-war-warning-for-india/

67   Jing, "How Does China Aim to Use AI in Warfare?".

68   Akashdeep Arul, "How China is using AI for Warfare", Analytics India, 21 Feb 2022, accessed on 15 Dec 2022.

https://analyticsindiamag.com/how-china-is-using-ai-for-warfare/

69   Meia Nouwens, "China's new Information Support Force", IISS, accessed on 20 May 2024.

https://www.iiss.org/en/online-analysis/online-analysis/2024/05/chinas-new-information-support-force/

70   Morgan et al., "Military Applications of Artificial Intelligence", p 66.

71   Amy J Nelson and Gerald L Epstein, "The PLA's Strategic Support Force and AI Innovation", Brookings, 23 Dec 2022, accessed on 08 Mar 2023.

https://www.brookings.edu/techstream/the-plas-strategic-support-force-and-ai-innovation-china-military-tech/

72   Jeirou Lee, "Artificial Intelligence Technology and China's Defense System", Journal of Indo-Pacific Affairs, Mar-Apr 2022, accessed on 15 Dec 2022.

https://media.defense.gov/2022/Mar/28/2002964034/1/1/1/FEATURE_LI.PDF

73   Stephen Chen, "Chinese AI plays war games like a human, with military strategists unable to identify it as a machine, developers say in Beijing", SCMP, 23 Feb 2023, accessed on 13 Mar 2023.

https://www.scmp.com/news/china/science/article/3211142/chinese-ai-plays-war-games-human-military-strategists-unable-identify-it-machine-say-developers

74   Elsa Kania, "Artificial Intelligence in Future Chinese Command Decision Making", Air University Press, accessed on 09 Mar 2023.

https://www.jstor.org/stable/pdf/resrep19585.26.pdf?refreqid=excelsior%3A28f037d2b7aaa39b25be6e923051aced&ab_segments=&origin=&initiator=&acceptTC=1

75   Morgan et al., "Military Applications of Artificial Intelligence", p 70.

76   Lee, "Artificial Intelligence Technology and China's Defense System".

77 Nelson and Epstein, "The PLA's Strategic Support Force and AI Innovation", ibid.

78 ibid.

79 Morgan et al., "Military Applications of Artificial Intelligence".

80 Arul, "How China is using AI for Warfare".

81 ANI, "China's PLA aims to leverage advanced technology for use of unmanned weapons, artificial intelligence, says report", Economic Times, 30 Jan 2023, Accessed on 08 Mar 2023.

    https://economictimes.indiatimes.com/news/defence/chinas-pla-aims-to-leverage-advanced-technology-for-use-of-unmanned-weapons-artificial-intelligence-says-report/articleshow/97431564.cms?from=mdr

82 Lee, "Artificial Intelligence Technology and China's Defense System".

83 Global Security, "Dark Sword (An-Jian)", accessed on 14 Feb 2023.

    https://www.globalsecurity.org/military/world/china/anjian.htm

84 Chen Chuanren, "New Chinese Armed UAV Project Unveiled", AIN Online,21 Feb 2018, accessed on 14 Mar 2023.

    https://www.ainonline.com/aviation-news/defense/2018-02-21/new-chinese-armed-uav-project-unveiled

85 Wikipedia, "Hongdu GJ-11", accessed on 14 Mar 2023.

    https://en.wikipedia.org/wiki/Hongdu_GJ-11

86 Morgan et al., "Military Applications of Artificial Intelligence".

87 Juan Ju, "Norinco's Sharp Claw I UGV in service with Chinese army", Janes,15 Apr 2020, accessed on 14 Mar 2023.

    https://www.janes.com/defence-news/news-detail/norincos-sharp-claw-i-ugv-in-service-with-chinese-army

88 Army Recognition, "Sharp Claw 2", accessed on 14 Mar 2023.

    https://www.armyrecognition.com/china_chinese_unmanned_aerial_ground_systems_uk/sharp_claw_2_ugv_6x6_unmanned_ground_vehicle_technical_data_sheet_specifications_pictures_video_11412165.html

89 Elsa B Kania, "Chinese Sub Commanders May Get AI Help for Decision-Making", Defense One, 12 Feb 2018, accessed on 08 Mar 2023.

https://www.defenseone.com/ideas/2018/02/chinese-sub-commanders-may-get-ai-help-decision-making/145906/

90 "Robotic boats making waves", Nature Research Custom Media, Shanghai University, accessed on 14 Mar 2023.

https://www.nature.com/articles/d42473-022-00140-y

91 Report, "China deploying 'en masse' underwater drones in Indian Ocean", Livemint, 31 Dec 2020, accessed on 14 Mar 2023.

https://www.livemint.com/news/india/china-deploying-en-masse-underwater-drones-in-indian-ocean-report-11609373452869.html

92 Wikipedia, "Buoyancy Engine", accessed on 14 Mar 2023.

https://en.wikipedia.org/wiki/Buoyancy_engine

93 Global Security, "D3000 USV", accessed on 14 Mar 2023.

https://www.globalsecurity.org/military/world/china/d3000.htm

94 Adam Bartley and Matthew Warren, "How Drone Submarines Are Turning The Seabed Into A Future Battlefield", The Conversation, 11 Oct 2023, accessed on 14 Mar 2024.

https://theconversation.com/how-drone-submarines-are-turning-the-seabed-into-a-future-battlefield-215338

95 Morgan et al., "Military Applications of Artificial Intelligence".

96 ANI, "China's PLA aims to leverage advanced technology for use of unmanned weapons, artificial intelligence, says report", Economic Times, 30 Jan 2023, Accessed on 08 Mar 2023.

https://economictimes.indiatimes.com/news/defence/chinas-pla-aims-to-leverage-advanced-technology-for-use-of-unmanned-weapons-artificial-intelligence-says-report/articleshow/97431564.cms?from=mdr

97 Kania, "Artificial Intelligence in Future Chinese Command Decision Making".

98 Stephen Chen, "In China, AI warship designer did nearly a year's work in a day",SCMP, 10 Mar 2023, accessed on 14 Mar 2023.

https://www.scmp.com/news/china/science/article/3213056/china-ai-warship-designer-did-nearly-years-work-day

99 Indian Aerospace Defence News (IADN) (@NewsIADN) tweeted at 1:26 AM on 14 Mar 2023,

https://twitter.com/NewsIADN/status/1635369382120673280?t=Q8fDFFQVY1TBmUjoc2obQA&s=03

100 Initiatives by MeitY in Emerging Technologies, accessed on 19 Apr 2024.

https://www.meity.gov.in/emerging-technologies-division

101 Press Release, "Cabinet Approves Ambitious IndiaAI Mission to Strengthen the AI Innovation Ecosystem", ID 2012375, Accessed 19 Apr 2024.

https://pib.gov.in/PressReleaseIframePage.aspx?PRID=2012355

102 PTI, "Cabinet approves India AI Mission with Rs 10,372 crore outlay", India Today, 7 Mar 2024, accessed on 20 Apr 2024.

https://www.indiatoday.in/business/story/cabinets-nod-to-india-ai-mission-with-outlay-of-rs-10372-crore-2512045-2024-03-07

103 Jim Garamone, "NATO Begins Largest Exercise Since Cold War", Defense, 25 Jan 2024, accessed on 13 Feb 2024.

https://www.defense.gov/News/NewsStories/Article/Article/3656703/nato-begins-largest-exercise-since-cold-war/#:~:text=The%20dock%20landing%20ship%20USS,reinforce%20the%20defense%20of%20Europe

104 "NATO's Steadfast Defender Exercises Mark Return to Cold War Schemes, Russia Says", US NEWS, 21 Jan 2024, accessed on 13 Feb 2024.

https://www.usnews.com/news/world/articles/2024-01-21/natos-steadfast-defender-exercises-mark-return-to-cold-war-schemes-russia-says

105 Jyoti Panday and Mila T Samdub, "Promises and Pitfalls of India's AI Industrial Policy", AI Now Institute, 12 Mar 2024, accessed on 20 Apr 2024.

https://ainowinstitute.org/wp-content/uploads/2024/03/AI-Nationalisms-Chapter-4.pdf

106 National Super Computing Mission, DST, accessed on 24 May 2024.

https://dst.gov.in/national-super-computing-mission#:~:text=National%20Supercomputing%20Mission%20(NSM)%20has,boost%20the%20country's%20computing%20power

107 Press Release, "Indian Air Force ushers in Digital Transformation with DigiLocker Integration", 26 Apr 2024, accessed on 20 May 2024.

https://pib.gov.in/PressReleasePage.aspx?PRID=2018958

108 Anirban Ghoshal, "India's advisory on LLM usage causes consternation", CIO, 05 Mar 2024, accessed on 20 Apr 2024.

https://www.cio.com/article/1311757/indias-advisory-on-llm-usage-causes-consternation.html

109 Presidential Address to the Federal Assembly at Saint Petersburg, Russia on 01 Mar 2018, accessed on 18 Feb 2023.

http://en.kremlin.ru/events/president/news/56957